Usborne Workbooks

Grammar
and
Punctuation

This book belongs to

....

There's a list of useful grammar and punctuation words on page 27, and notes for grown-ups at the back of the book.

Here are some of the woodland animals you'll meet in this book.
Trace over their capital letters.

Help the animals with their grammar and punctuation in this book.
You can draw, trace and write on each page.

Usborne Workbooks
Grammar and Punctuation

Illustrated by Maddie Frost

Written by Jessica Greenwell
Designed by Maddison Warnes

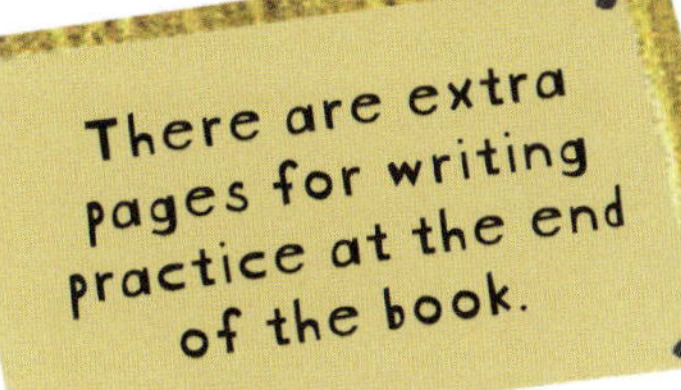

Edited by Hannah Watson
and Kristie Pickersgill
Series Editor: Felicity Brooks

Matching capital letters

Help the animals write capital letters to match these lower-case letters. You can use the alphabet at the bottom of the page to help you.

Spike

A	B	C		
a	b	c	d	e
f	g	h	i	j
k	l	m	n	
o	p	q	r	
s	t	u	v	w
x	y	z		

Moley

Mo

Can you say all of the letter sounds out loud?

Days of the week

Stripe is writing about the week. Can you help? Write capital letters over the grey letters, then add a full stop at the end of each sentence.

On Monday we played in the forest.

tuesday was a warm and sunny day

we went swimming on wednesday

on thursday we had a party

it rained all day on friday

we built a den on saturday

tomorrow it will be sunday

Sentences always start with a capital letter.
Days of the week start with a capital letter, too.
Sentences often end with a full stop.

Names and places

Trace the capital letters on these holiday pictures, then copy the words to complete the sentences under each picture.

__________ went to __________.

__________ went to __________.

__________ went to __________.

You can use the alphabet strip at the bottom of the page to check your capital letters.

Names and places always begin with a capital letter.
The personal pronoun 'I' always has a capital letter, too.

_________ went to _________.

_________ went to _________.

_________ went to _________.

_________ went to _________.

Countries, cities, towns and villages all start with a capital letter. Think of a city, town or village you have visited and complete the sentence below.

I went to _________.

Punctuation marks

Trace over these punctuation marks, then see if you can write some more below.

Sentences usually end with a full stop.

Questions always end with a question mark.

Exclamation marks end sentences that show strong feelings.

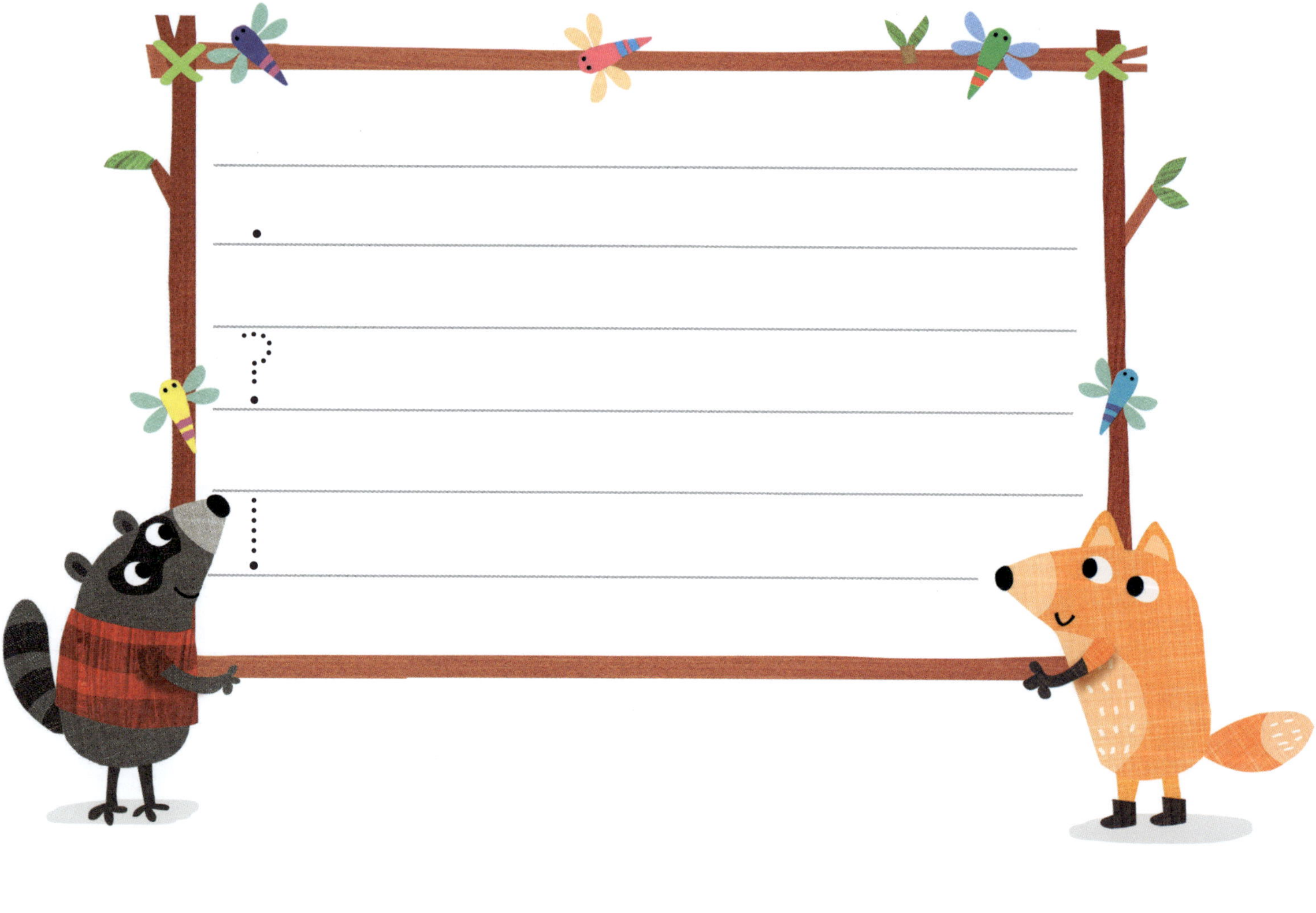

Olly is asking questions. Add a question mark to each of his sentences.

Squilly is answering Olly's questions. Add a full stop to each of his sentences.

Hug is trying to sleep. Add an exclamation mark to each of his sentences.

Punctuating sentences

Add punctuation marks to these sentences, then draw lines to show each animal where they need to land.

Coco has written a party invitation, but she's forgotten to use punctuation. Write in the missing full stops, question marks and exclamation marks.

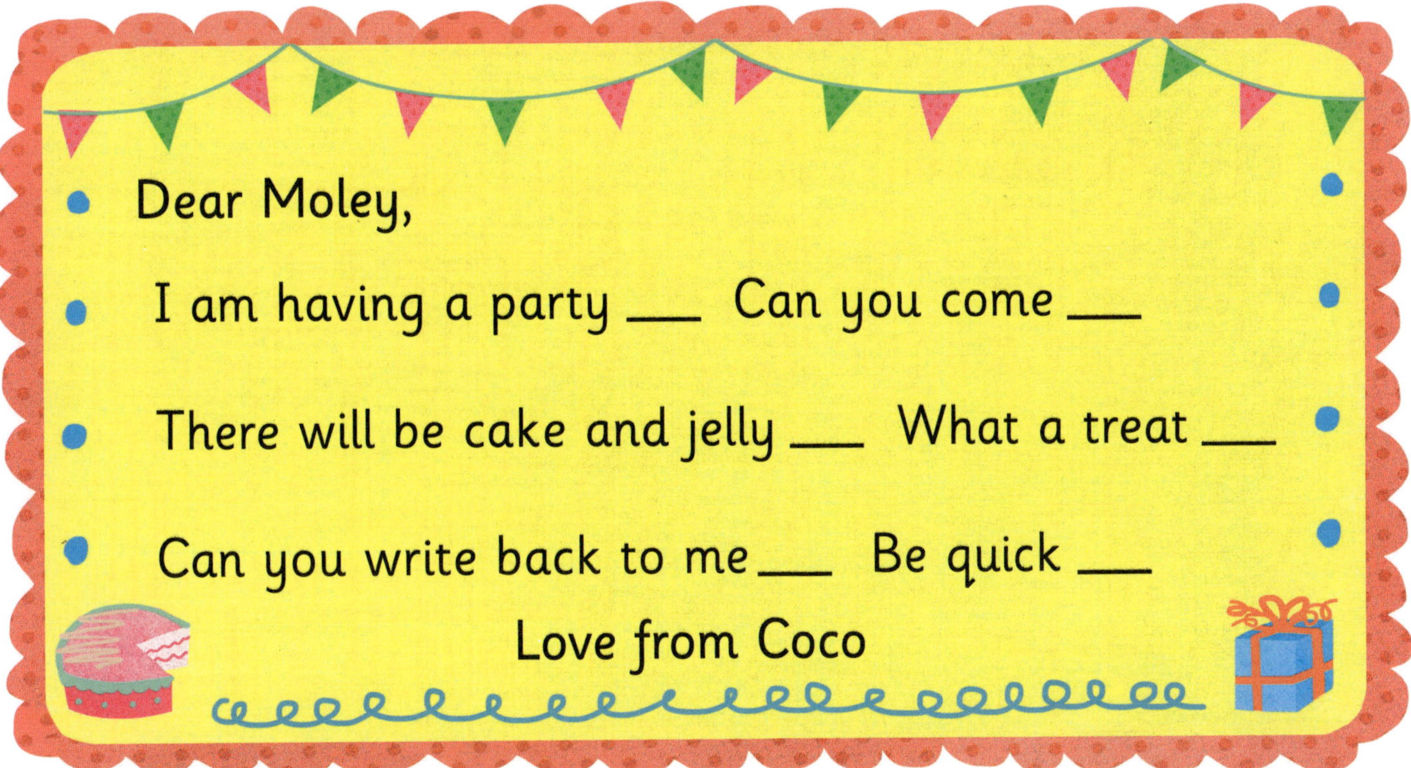

Moley has written back to Coco. Add the missing punctuation marks to her letter.

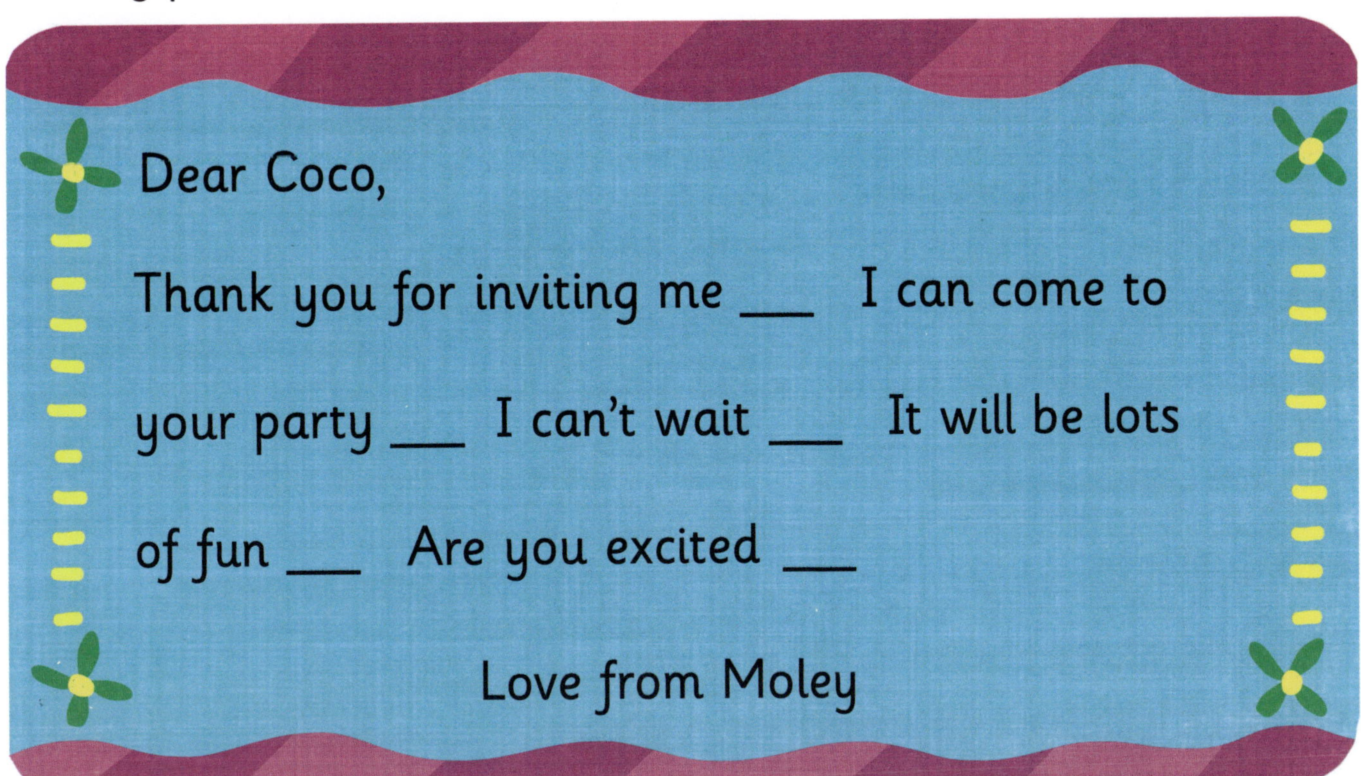

Making sentences

Draw lines to join the parts of these sentences so that they make sense, and see which animal is going by bike, car or boat.

I drive

ride my bike.

I am going

a green car.

I want to

sailing.

Copy the words from the clouds to write sentences on the planes' banners.

Put Mo's train wagons in order for her by writing out the words to make a sentence.

Muddled pages

Squilly is putting together pages for a book. Help him unscramble the words to make sentences. Write the sentences under the pictures, then put the pages in order by writing 1, 2, 3 or 4 in the boxes.

A

rabbit.

squirrel

met

a

They

always

will

friends.

be

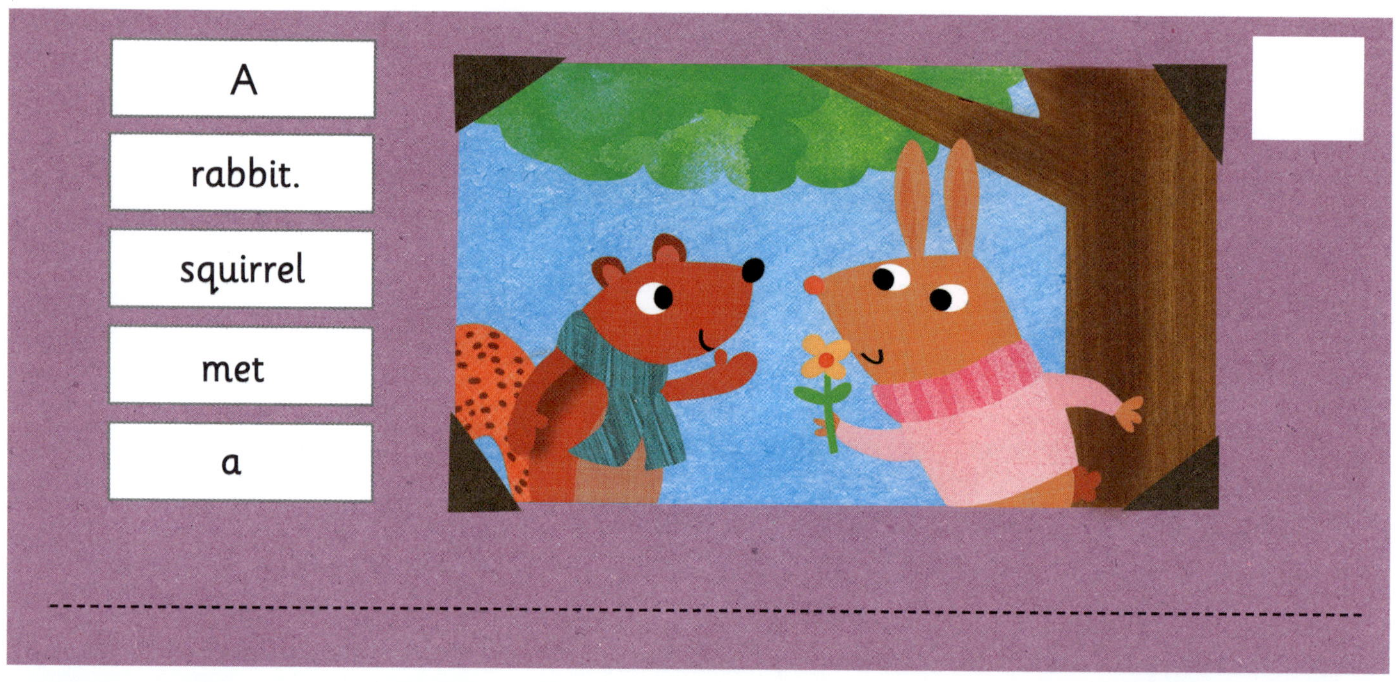

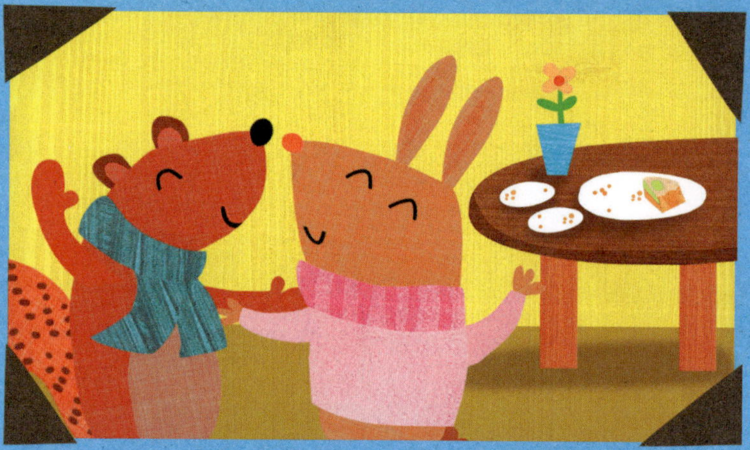

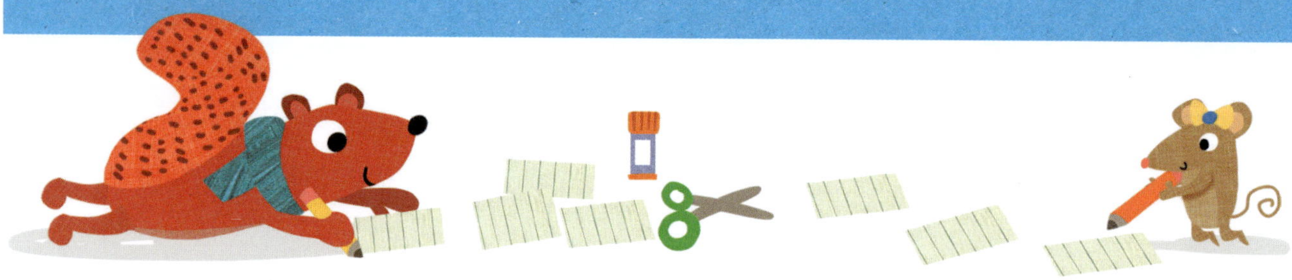

Remember to start your sentences with a capital letter and end with a full stop.

Then

pie.

apple

they

ate

They

treehouse.

in

played

the

Linking sentences

Read the sentences in the boxes, then draw a piece of string to link them together. Turn each pair into one new sentence by writing 'and' in the space. The mice have done the first one for you.

Stripe likes to eat fruit.   Stripe likes to eat nuts.

Stripe likes to eat fruit **and** nuts.

Bun is happy.   Bun is excited.

Bun is happy   excited.

Bun and Stripe are singing.   Bun and Stripe are dancing.

Bun and Stripe are singing   dancing.

Bun is reading.   Stripe is sleeping.

Bun is reading   Stripe is sleeping.

Rewrite what each animal is saying
in one new sentence using 'and'.

I am ____

I love ____

The butterfly is ____

I am playing with ____

One or more than one?

Help Olly tidy away his toys. Draw a line from each label to the correct box.

Can you write labels for Olly's toys? Trace each word and add 's' to make it plural.

ball __   pen __   robot __

These words need 'es' to make them plural.

fox __ __   watch __ __   bus __ __

Draw around the singular words in the wordsearch to match these pictures.

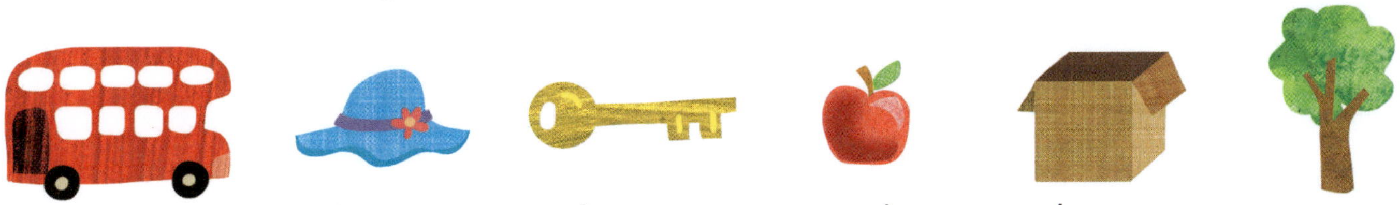

bus

hat

key

apple

box

tree

a	k	e	y	s	b
c	p	m	n	b	u
a	a	p	l	o	s
r	v	x	l	x	e
s	t	r	e	e	s
v	h	a	t	s	s

Find a pen or pencil that's a different colour.

Now draw around the plural words to match these pictures.

buses

hats

keys

apples

boxes

trees

Changing words

Trace the words below and then write 'un' in the spaces to make new words.

dress   __ __ dress

tie   __ __ tie

zip   __ __ zip

Trace these words and then write 'ing' in the spaces to make new words.

mix

paint

cook

listen

play

jump

Now trace the words below and write 'ed' after each one.
Think about how this changes the meaning of the word.

mix

cook

play

paint

listen

jump

Writing practice

The animals are practising writing sentences, but they've missed a few things out. Write the sentences out correctly for them.

we went swimming on wednesday

are you excited

spike went to italy

can you write back to me

bun and stripe like to sing dance

my train fast goes

how exciting

Now try writing your own sentences about the animals in this picture.
There are some words at the bottom of the page to give you some ideas.

singing   writing   fun   lunch   picture   song
painting   eating   sleeping   yummy   book

Grammar and punctuation quiz

Find out how much you can remember about grammar
and punctuation by doing this quiz. Answers on page 26.

1. Tick one word that completes this **sentence.**

Yesterday Stripe and Moley __________ in the forest.

a) playing ☐   b) play ☐   c) played ☐   d) plays ☐

2. Write one **punctuation mark** in each box to complete these **sentences.**

a) Are we nearly there ☐   d) Be quiet ☐

b) Stripe likes sausages ☐   e) Are you awake ☐

c) What noisy animals ☐   f) Foxy is in America ☐

3. Tick one **word** that completes this **sentence.**

Bun and Stripe are singing ________ dancing.

a) and ☐   b) but ☐

c) so ☐   d) because ☐

4. Tick one box to show if you add 's' or 'es' to make each of these words **plural**.

	's'	'es'
a) fox	☐	☐
b) bus	☐	☐
c) key	☐	☐

5. Tick one box to show which **letters** you need to add to this **sentence.**

Squilly has to __ zip his jacket before he takes it off.

a) under ☐

b) un ☐

c) out ☐

6. Draw a line under each **letter** that should be a **capital letter** in this story, then tick one box to show how many capitals are missing.

coco went to france on tuesday. she met her friend bun in paris. they came back on friday. i would like to go to paris too.

a) 8 ☐   b) 5 ☐   c) 10 ☐   d) 12 ☐

Write out the story again with capital letters in the right places.

....

....

....

....

26

7. Write 'ed' or 'ing' in the spaces to complete these **sentences.**

a) Foxy likes listen _______ to music.

b) Hug cook _____ a yummy pie for Olly's birthday.

c) Coco and Bun are play _______ with their toys.

d) Spike paint _______ a picture for Olly.

8. Write out the words in the right order to unmuddle these sentences. Add **capital letters** and **full stops** too.

a)   green spike drives car a

....

b)   going is moley sailing

....

c)   bike ride foxy his to wants

....

Quiz answers

1. c)   2. a) ? b) . c) ! d) ! e) ? f) .   3. a)   4. a) 'es' b) 'es' c) 's'   5. b)

6. c) (1 point)   7. a) listening b) cooked c) playing d) painted

Coco went to France on Tuesday.   8. a) Spike drives a green car.
She met her friend Bun in Paris.
They came back on Friday.   b) Moley is going sailing.
I would like to go to Paris too.
                                                          c) Foxy wants to ride his bike.

Score 1 point for each correct answer and write your score in this box: 20

Grammar and punctuation words

capital letter – a big letter of the alphabet that you use at the beginning of sentences, names, places, days of the week and months of the year. You also need a capital letter when you are talking about yourself using the word 'I'.

exclamation mark – a punctuation mark (!) you use at the end of a sentence to show a strong emotion, such as surprise or excitement.

full stop – a punctuation mark (.) you use at the end of a sentence to mark a pause.

letter – a character in the alphabet that is used to spell words.

plural – more than one of something. When a word is plural it normally ends in 's' or 'es'.

punctuation – the marks, such as full stops, commas, exclamation marks and question marks, that you use in writing to separate sentences and make them easier to understand.

question mark – a punctuation mark (?) that you use at the end of a question to show that it is asking something.

sentence – a group of words that makes sense on its own and ends in a punctuation mark.

singular – just one of something.

word – a group of letters with its own meaning, used with others to make a sentence.

You can use
these pages for
writing practice.

You could practise writing your name on this page.

Don't forget to use a capital letter.

Don't forget to use capital letters and punctuation.

Here you could write a diary entry about what you've done today.

What could the
animals be saying? Use
full sentences to fill in
their speech bubbles.

Notes for grown-ups

Matching capital letters/Days of the week (pages 4–5)

This allows children to practise writing upper-case letters and matching them to their lower-case counterparts. They can see how capital letters are used for days of the week and at the beginning of sentences. Encourage children to think about other times when a capital letter is used.

Names and places (pages 6–7)

This provides further practice in using capital letters at the start of proper nouns, such as names and places, and introduces the need for a capital letter for the personal pronoun 'I'. Children could use the blank pages at the back of the book to write new sentences with other personal pronouns or with their name.

Punctuation marks (pages 8–9)

These activities show how full stops, question marks and exclamation marks are used to punctuate sentences. They introduce children to different sentence types (statements, questions, exclamations) as they are prompted to fill in the missing punctuation marks.

Punctuating sentences (pages 10–11)

This gives children more practice in using full stops, question marks and exclamation marks to punctuate sentences. Children can decide which punctuation marks are needed to complete longer phrases, and could try writing their own sentences with punctuation on the blank pages at the back of the book.

Making sentences (pages 12–13)

This helps children understand how sentences are structured and practise correct word order by sorting jumbled words. They may realize that they can use the placement of capital letters and full stops as clues to work out the correct word order of a sentence.

Muddled pages (pages 14–15)

This activity reinforces the correct word order of a sentence as children unscramble words to make a story. Children can order the parts of a story to form a logical narrative. You could ask children to explain how they were able to use clues in the text to work out the word order.

Linking sentences (pages 16–17)

This introduces the use of the conjunction 'and' to link clauses and form more complex sentences. Children can practise filling in the missing 'and' and writing whole sentences using 'and'.

One or more than one? (pages 18–19)

This explores the concepts of singular and plural. Children can recognize singular and plural words, and add the right ending to a singular word to make it plural.

Changing words (pages 20–21)

This introduces the prefix 'un-' as a way to modify the meaning of a verb. It also introduces the suffixes '-ing' and '-ed' as a way to signal which tense a verb is in. You could encourage children to think about how the prefix 'un-', and the suffixes '-ing' and '-ed' change the meaning of a word.

Writing practice (pages 22–23)

These pages give children an opportunity to recap the grammar points covered in the book, including capital letters, punctuation marks, word order, linking words, and words with '-ing'. There is space for children to write their own sentences, too.